A WEEK OF FAITH
MORE PRECIOUS
THAN GOLD

Seven Short Stories and Devotionals

Lynn Squire

"That the trial of your faith, being much more precious than of gold that perisheth, though it be tried with fire, might be found unto praise and honour and glory at the appearing of Jesus Christ."

I Peter 1:7

Faith Journey Books
www.faithjourneybooks.com

A Week of Faith More Precious than Gold
by Lynn Squire
edited by Marjorie Vawter, Shevet Writing Services

Faith Journey Books, an imprint of Home, Hobbies, and Asundry

All scripture quotations are from the King James Version (KJV) of the Bible. Public Domain.

The short stories in this book are works of fiction. Names, characters, places, and incidents are either products of the author's imagination or used fictitiously.

ISBN 13: **978-0615553788** (Faith Journey Books)
ISBN 10: **0615553788**

Printed in the United States of America

DEDICATION

The desire to compile this book came as a result of discussions with my critique group, the ReadyPens. To you, my faithful friends, do I dedicate this book.

CONTENTS

ACKNOWLEDGMENTS

To the readers of FaithFictionFunandFanciful.blogspot.com, thank you for your encouraging comments.

To my husband and my children, thank you for putting up with my long hours and hair-pulling moments as I compiled this book.

To my Lord and Saviour, without You, there is no purpose in living.

To Calvary Baptist Church, American Canyon, California, my home and my family, thank you for all your faithful support and Godly teaching.

INTRODUCTION

Often referred to as the chapter of faith, Hebrews 11 gives us examples of men and women in the Bible who lived by faith. These people inspire us to not look at our present circumstances and the pleasures of sin, but to esteem "the reproach of Christ greater" (Hebrews 11:26).

Throughout history men and women have followed that example and have proven that indeed "faith is the substance of things hoped for, the evidence of things not seen" (Hebrews 11:1) and have kept their focus on eternity.

Martyrs recognized that the choices they made would ultimately prove their faith. They loved the Lord and sought to please Him. On their day of truth, they understood Hebrews 11:6 at a level few people ever will.

> "But without faith it is impossible to please him: for he that cometh to God must believe that he is, and that he is a rewarder of them that diligently seek him."
>
> Hebrews 11:6

The stories and devotionals in this booklet focus on people who gave their lives for their faith. Some stories, like "Arnoldo" and "And Then Came Peace," evolved from

1

studying true stories of martyrs. Others are purely fictional, though the struggles the characters face are the same many readers may face today.

Time is a precious commodity. Yet, each day we need to dedicate our time to our Lord and Saviour. When I planned *A Week of Faith More Precious than Gold*, I wanted to give my readers tales that will help strengthen their faith and draw their focus to the Lord. In particular, I desired to give my readers trigger stories and questions that would encourage them to study God's Word. You can use this book for your own personal study, perhaps take it on vacation with you, or you can use it for your women's Bible study group.

I pray that through these stories you will be inspired by the courage of faithful men and women to endure all trials you may face and find the unspeakable joy and fullness of glory the Apostle Peter speaks of in I Peter 1:6–16. May the Lord bless you and draw you closer to Him as you graze on the stories and the food for thought questions.

"Wherein ye greatly rejoice, though now for a season, if need be, ye are in heaviness through manifold temptations:

That the trial of your faith, being much more precious than of gold that perisheth, though it be tried with fire, might be found unto praise and honour and glory at the appearing of Jesus Christ:

Whom having not seen, ye love; in whom, though now ye see him not, yet believing, ye rejoice with joy unspeakable and full of glory:

Receiving the end of your faith, even the salvation of your souls.

Of which salvation the prophets have enquired and searched diligently, who prophesied of the grace that should come unto you:

Searching what, or what manner of time the Spirit of Christ which was in them did signify, when it testified beforehand the sufferings of Christ, and the glory that should follow.

Unto whom it was revealed, that not unto themselves, but unto us they did minister the things, which are now reported unto you by them that have preached the gospel unto you with the Holy Ghost sent down from heaven; which things the angels desire to look into.

Wherefore gird up the loins of your mind, be sober, and hope to the end for the grace that is to be brought unto you at the revelation of Jesus Christ;

As obedient children, not fashioning yourselves according to the former lusts in your ignorance:

But as he which hath called you is holy, so be ye holy in all manner of conversation;

Because it is written, Be ye holy; for I am holy."

I Peter 1:6–16

ARNOLDO

Brescia, Italy 1139

"They gain their wealth at the hands of the poor!" the bald man dressed in a monk's habit shouted from a wooden crate in the main street of Brescia. "The Romish Church has no right to own property."

With one voice, the crowd revealed their reverence of him, but Theresa stood by the door of her father's blacksmith shop pondering his sanity. Did not this man realize he was inciting his own death?

The smell of fish and sweaty bodies rode on the breeze, swirling through the market like a stirred stew of stench.

Theresa's fist tightened around the scroll handed to her by the monk's disciple. Perhaps she was playing the fool now. Would she be killed for bearing a message?

"He studied in France," a passerby whispered as he bumped Theresa's shoulder.

She draped her scarf over her head and across her face.

"He claims the Church does not have the right to rule as a kingdom," another whispered in return.

Theresa ducked under a farmer's canopy and slipped past another.

4

"The sacraments the Church practices are not as written in Scripture!" The man, lifted a book in his hand. "Convert and be baptized again!"

"Arnoldo!" Theresa hissed as she drew up behind him. "I have a message."

The monk stepped down from the crate and pulled on his beard. "What is it?"

Theresa pressed the scroll into his hand. "You must leave. The count-bishop is preparing his coaches. He plans to take you to the pope."

The *clop-clop* of prancing hooves on cobblestone confirmed her words, and the anxious neighing of high-strung horses rose above the crowd's murmurs.

Theresa's shoulder's rounded, and she ducked back from the crate.

Arnoldo looked across the market. "I see you are right. That is his impressive vehicle now, is it not?"

"Yes. Please, come with me." She turned and lifted the hem of her skirts from the filthy cobblestone. "I know a way to the Alps where he will not dare follow . . . not in a coach."

"But to run . . ."

"To run is to save your life and perhaps give you opportunity to share the truth with many more."

Her words seemed to convince him for he grabbed her elbow and waved her on. They weaved through the merchant canopies that lined the street. These hovered over her as though a net sent by Satan to capture them.

She pressed her hand against her throbbing chest and ducked under another tent.

"There he runs!" the count-bishop barked.

"Down here." Theresa gestured to a stairwell.

"Follow them!" Pounding boots drew close.

"Lord Jesus, help us," she whispered as her hand followed the rough stone wall.

The monk breathed heavily at her side. He maneuvered the crumbling steps with some effort.

"We've not far." She gripped his elbow and led him down a dark corridor. For years her family had used this passage to escape the attacks of the Lombards on their city. Now, Lord willing, it would provide a way of escape for Arnoldo.

Footsteps echoed against the stone walls, being carried by the cool air of the passage.

Theresa shivered and urged the monk forward to what appeared to be a dead end.

"We've nowhere to go." He panted.

She ran her hand along the wall until she felt the familiar star-shaped stone and pressed it.

A quiet creaking announced the slow movement of the wall. Earthy air slipped through and surrounded them.

She pushed the monk into the black corridor and glanced back before following him.

The bishop's men had not yet reached the head of the corridor.

She tugged on a heavy cord and the wall moved back into place. If God be with them, the men would not see the wall move.

"It's so dark."

"Ssh." She grabbed the monk's hand and lifted her other hand to the cold stone beside her. Sliding her foot to the base of the wall, she inched along it.

For a hundred feet they shuffled then rounded a turn, and a light the size of a pinhead shone at the end.

"You'll need to get on your hands and knees. The ceiling lowers before we reach the exit." Theresa dropped to the dirt floor.

A whiff of onion and body odor floated by as the rough wool of the monk's garb rubbed against her hand.

She tugged his wool garment, halting his movement. "Grab my foot, and I'll guide you."

They crawled one after the other for several feet while the light grew until blue sky could be seen through a hole the size of a bear's waist.

"Praise be to God." She let the words escape on a breath. "Pray that none of the bishop's men are on the other side."

The monk's heavy breathing echoed through the narrow passageway.

The grit of the floor pressed into Theresa's hands, and her knees bled against her skirt. If things went as planned, her brother, Joseph, would be waiting with horses. She held her breath as she peered out through the hole.

"Pst!"

With a start, she turned and saw her brother holding two bays. "The bishop's men have come through the city gates. We must hurry," he said, trotting up to her with the horses in hand.

Theresa pointed to the scroll in the monk's hand and fixed her gaze on the monk's sweaty face. "That is a letter of introduction. My father has a friend in Zurich with whom you will stay. My brother will take you as far as Liechtenstein. There you will be given further directions."

"God be with you." The monk bowed his head to her.

"And you."

Shouts rode upon the wind.

They were like nettles pricking her nerves.

"The guards are coming." Joseph helped the monk onto the smaller bay. "Theresa, go back."

She dove into the hole and held her breath as she listened to the thunder of horses' hooves fade. *God of mercy, help them. Keep them safe.*

The sun began to set before Theresa left her post and made her way back down the dark tunnel. By the time she left the corridors, darkness had engulfed the town of Brescia. She stepped out into the street, pulling her hood over her head and around her face.

"Theresa!" a man rasped.

She rushed to the voice. "Father."

He took her hands and pulled her into a dark building. "Did he get away? Did Joseph make it?"

"Yes."

He nodded and looked across the alley. "He was Brescia's hope, you know." He ran his hand through his thinning hair. "Heaven beheld Italia's tears and sent us Arnoldo. God be praised."

"Jacob."

Theresa slipped behind her father. She didn't recognize the voice. Who could it be?

"Eugenius, what is the word?" Her father drew his arm around her and placed her beside him. "This is my daughter. She led Arnoldo to Joseph."

The tall man with dark robes and a hood that hid his face nodded to her. "My pigeon brought word they made it to Liechtenstein." He rested a hand on Jacob's shoulder. "They're safe and Joseph will return in the morrow."

Theresa felt her father's arm relax, though her own body trembled with fatigue.

"God be praised," her father replied and led her to a chair.

Energy whooshed from her like air from an oilskin sack. God had spared them. By God's grace, Arnoldo would continue to speak of the freedom found in Christ. Perhaps she had not been such a fool to help him after all.

Bro. Arnoldo continued to preach the true Gospel of the free gift of salvation. He later returned to Rome, convincing many of their freedom, but when he retired to Tuscany, he was seized. Taken to Rome, he was condemned by the Pope who had him crucified and burned, and his ashes thrown into the Tiber. [1]

While it may appear as though the clergy won, Arnoldo's followers continued his message of preaching the true Gospel of Christ. Unlike those clergy who did not believe that one is saved by faith in the death, burial, and

---

[1] J. Newton Brown, Memorials of Baptist Martyrs (Philadelphia: American Baptist Publication Society, 1854) 40–42.

resurrection of Jesus Christ, Arnoldo now finds his rest in Heaven, with other martyrs of the faith.

Food for Thought

1. How does one get saved? Read Romans 10:9–13.

> "That if thou shalt confess with thy mouth the Lord Jesus, and shalt believe in thine heart that God hath raised him from the dead, thou shalt be saved. For with the heart man believeth unto righteousness; and with the mouth confession is made unto salvation. For the scripture saith, Whosoever believeth on him shall not be ashamed. For there is no difference between the Jew and the Greek: for the same Lord over all is rich unto all that call upon him. For whosoever shall call upon the name of the Lord shall be saved."
>
> Romans 10:9–13

2. Does the Bible warn us of those who teach false doctrine? Read Paul's epistle to the Galatians; I Timothy 4:1–5; II Timothy 3:1–9; II Peter 2.

> "Now the Spirit speaketh expressly, that in the latter times some shall depart from the faith, giving heed to seducing spirits, and doctrines of devils; speaking lies in hypocrisy; having their conscience seared with a hot iron; forbidding to marry, and commanding to abstain from meats, which God hath created to be received with thanksgiving of them which believe and know the truth. For every creature of God is good, and nothing to be refused, if it be received with thanksgiving: For it is sanctified by the word of God and prayer."
>
> I Timothy 4:1-5

3. If you lived in a time and a place where you could be killed for sharing God's true Gospel, would you have the courage to do so? Read Philippians 1.

> "For I know that this shall turn to my salvation through your prayer, and the supply of the Spirit of Jesus Christ, according to my earnest expectation and my hope, that in nothing I shall be ashamed, but that with all boldness, as always, so now also Christ shall be magnified in my body, whether it be by life, or by death. For to me to live is Christ, and to die is gain. But if I live in the flesh, this is the fruit of my labour: yet what I shall choose I wot not. For I am in a strait betwixt two, having a desire to depart, and to be with Christ; which is far better: Nevertheless to abide in the flesh is more needful for you."
>
> Philippians 1:19–24

The Apostle Paul did not fear death. However, he saw the importance of living to tell others how they too can no longer fear death.

ADARA'S HOPE

Ephesus, 1st Century

With a blanket thrown over her shoulders, Adara sank to the cobblestones behind Belen's baskets. Her hands shook as she recalled her mother's words. "If you defy me on this, Adara, I will reveal your conversion, and you know you'll be hunted down."

Adara squeezed her arms around her body. Her mother had leaned close and whispered, "The lions are hungry." But Adara had insisted on going to the meeting at Eunice's home. Her mother would do as she said, for she hated Christians.

Belen's merchant tent had seemed the only safe retreat in all of Ephesus. Now, listening to the shouts of soldiers and the thunder of marching feet, she realized she'd not thought it through. She hadn't considered the danger in which she'd placed him.

Hurried footsteps came toward the canopy. More shouts rose above the crowd.

She held her breath and tugged on the blanket, making sure it covered her.

Belen's bare feet shuffled by. "Pomegranates? Fresh olives from the finest trees in all of Asia," he called.

She could hear the quiver in his voice, and it made her stomach churn. Why had she done it? Why did she cross her mother and become a Christian?

The scent of fish crept under the blanket.

She waved her hand in front of her nose. Doubt must not enter her heart, or she truly would be lost.

Belen's foot bumped her head. It smelled of sweat and rotten fruit. "Adara," he hissed. "Go."

Adara ripped the blanket off and looked up at the dark man with curly short hair. He could have been Caesar; his features were so Roman. "But what of you? I've endangered you."

"Don't worry about me. Your mother has turned you in, not me."

Adara glanced down the street, a maze of canopies with merchants shouting and calling to those around them. She grabbed Belen's arm. How could she leave him there, knowing that her mother would blame him for her conversion? "You should come with me. Your life—it's not safe."

He patted her arm and gave her a tight smile. "You must go to the river. Timothy is there. He'll baptize you. Quickly. The guards will be back this way." He gave her a gentle shove. "Now go. I'll see you again."

From the corner of her eye she caught the plume of a temple guard's helmet. Belen must have seen it too, for he whirled her around and pushed her away.

Like the march of a centurion, her heart pounded in her chest. She pulled her shawl over her head and hurried into the crowd. God must protect Belen and help her now.

Animal dung, spices, wine—all these scents she passed as she weaved in and out of the men, women, and children milling through the marketplace. Elbows banged her. An angry merchant shouted as she knocked over a basket of wool. She stumbled over uneven ground and pushed through a crowd of young men lounging by the Magnesian Gate.

Dropping behind a rosemary bush, she gasped for breath. "What now, God?"

Her mother's words still rang in her ears. "Traitor!" She had curled her lips in disgust when she spat out, "Christian."

"Why didn't I keep my mouth shut?" Adara sobbed into her hands. She should have known her mother would hate her, but she had hoped and prayed that her mom might want to know this Hebrew God who had sacrificed Himself for them.

Pain rose in her constricting chest. She should never have listened to Belen that day, six weeks ago. If she had turned her back on him that morning . . .

She groaned. The handsome merchant had offered her more than pomegranates. She had pointed to the symbol of a fish carved into the post of his booth, a symbol used by Christians to identify themselves.

He had smiled. Oh, what a wonderful smile, so pure, so inviting. He had asked if she knew what the fish symbol was.

That simple little touch of curiosity brought her here, a fugitive outside this gate to Ephesus.

She grasped a fistful of dirt and flung it across the road. No doubt she would die now.

I am the resurrection and the life.

"Yes Lord, but what of now?" She pressed the heels of her hands against her eyes. "What of life, home, and family?"

He that finds his life shall lose it: and he that loses his life shall find it.

"But how can I know for sure what I am doing is right?"

Trust and obey.

She bent forward and wept. The peace she found when Belen shared with her the life of Christ was like nothing she had ever experienced before. The joy—she wiped her tears and her heart swelled. Yes, even now the joy was real.

A tingling sensation crept up her arms and pushed past her neck. The joy she knew was like none found in the temple of Artemis.

Her face burst into a smile. "Oh my Lord and Saviour, You who saved me, thank You."

She buried her face in her hands. "Forgive me for my lack of faith."

Her legs shook as she stood, but in her heart came strength greater than the pillars of the Temple of Artemis. "I will go, Lord. I will go to the river, find Timothy, and be baptized."

She stepped out on the road with an energy surpassing that of the tide. Her legs, light with joy, raced her down the road and along the Cayster River. Today she would identify herself fully with the Christians and prove her acceptance of the life she found in Christ...even if it meant eventual death by the mouth of a lion.

Food For Thought

1. How can you remain faithful when people threaten to kill you for your faith?

During the Apostolic Age and throughout history to this present time, men and women have faced death for what they believed. Their faith, however, empowered them to stand before those who hated them, those who had the power to save their lives should they renounce their faith.

What kept them from giving up? Hope. When Paul stood before King Agrippa he said in his defense, "And now I stand and am judged for the hope of the promise made of God unto our fathers:" Acts 26:6. In times of persecution, when his life was on the line, Paul endured because he had that blessed hope of eternal life.

Today many of us may never face the firing squad, or be burned at the stake, or have our homes destroyed because of what we believe, but we may experience pressure to compromise. At those moments, when someone mocks us, we need to be as the witnesses who lived before us, and stand firm. The hope we have in Christ is sure and worth more than popularity, more than acceptance by man. Christ gave us that hope with His life, should we not then be willing to give up our lives for Him?

> "For we are saved by hope: but hope that is seen is not hope: for what a man seeth, why doth he yet hope for? But if we hope for that we see not, then do we with patience wait for it."
>
> Romans 8:24–25

2. When Adara went to Timothy to be baptized, what statement was she making?

Baptism is a form of identification. When you are baptized you are identifying yourself with a group. A person who is baptized as a Catholic is Catholic. A person who is baptized as an Anglican is Anglican. Ephesians 4:5, however, tells us that there is only one baptism: "One Lord, one faith, one baptism."

The New Testament Church baptized by immersion. To study more about baptism, read the following passages of Scripture: Matthew 3:1, 6–8, 13–17; 11:11; 28:19–20; Mark 1:10; John 3:23, 4:1; 14:15; Acts 1:22; 2:38–42; 8:12, 37–39; 10:47; 16:14,15, 30–34; 18:8; Romans 6:4–5, 17–18; I Corinthians 12:13; 15:1–4; Colossians 2:12; I Peter 3:21.

> "And as they went on their way, they came unto a certain water: and the eunuch said, See, here is water; what doth hinder me to be baptized? **And Philip said, If thou believest with all thine heart, thou mayest. And he answered and said, I believe that Jesus Christ is the Son of God.** And he commanded the chariot to stand still: and they went down both

into the water, both Philip and the eunuch; and he baptized him. And when they were come up out of the water, the Spirit of the Lord caught away Philip, that the eunuch saw him no more: and he went on his way rejoicing."

Acts 8:36–39

2. Did Adara receive salvation before she was baptized or after?

According to Ephesians 2:8, we are saved by grace, not by baptism.

"For by grace are ye saved through faith; and that not of yourselves: it is the gift of God: not of works, lest any man should boast."

Ephesians 2:8–9

Baptism does not save you. If it did then verse 9 above would be a lie, but since the Bible speaks the truth, then no work, not even baptism, can save you.

For further study look up Luke 23:32–43; John 17:17; Ephesians 5:26; Titus 3:5; and Revelation 1:5; 7:14.

AND THEN CAME PEACE

Switzerland, 17th Century

Hans stared across the frozen Aare River at Berne, and shivers ran up his spine, but not from the cold. Martin had insisted on meeting him by the old plum tree. Something about protecting family. Something guaranteed to get Hans's family in trouble, no doubt.

The State Church had sent Benner and Hummel to stop their last meeting only two days earlier. At this early hour, however, no one yet appeared along the paths and roads.

Shooting a nervous glance upstream, Hans banged his mitted hands together. This rendezvous would only lead to trouble. Why did he let himself get into these situations?

"Hans," whispered Martin.

Hans looked over his shoulder to see the skinny farmer huddled in the snow behind a bush. No doubt he'd not eaten in days.

With another quick scan of the riverbanks, Hans's heart sped. The price of being caught with a known Anabaptist...well, he'd never see his family again. Ack, why did he have such a soft heart and addled brain? "Martin, you fool. What is it you want?"

"My children, I hope to protect them from the abbot. Venner and Hummel came to my farm last night. They seek to expel me"—Martin rubbed his grizzly beard—"and the others."

"Old news." Hans grunted. Those zealot minions of the abbot thought to expel anyone who didn't scratch their itch on a daily basis. Nonetheless, the danger was real. "I'm not your brother. Why should I risk my own neck for you?"

"I know you to be a good man, a man of integrity, and you do not hold to the ways of the State Church. You should convert, abandon the legal traps the abbot sets for those he deceives, and be saved."

"I hold not to the morality of those who run the church, but who am I to deny God?" How was a man, such as himself, to know for sure that going against the traditions of the church would be right?

"There is no spiritual life under the abbot." Martin inched away from the bush and rose to his full, lanky height. He held his felt hat in his hand and ran his fingers along its brim, a nervous habit Hans had learned to identify as Martin's way to strengthen his resolve.

Hans rubbed his nose. "True." This abbot seemed to have no conscience.

The sun had risen over the eastern horizon, but its rays did little to take the chill from the air.

A nervous huff escaped Hans's nostrils. With the sun up, they would soon be discovered. "How can I possibly help you and your family? I am no knight that can hold at bay the abbot's own guard."

"On your property is a cave. Within it we could hide supplies, things our families need in order to escape the coming cruelties."

A cave did exist, but only those close to him knew the entrance. "How did you learn of this?"

"I have ears and eyes." Martin placed his hat on his head. "You seek peace, but you will not find it in ignoring the evil acts of this State Church."

"What do you know of my desires?"

"I read it in your eyes." Martin poked Hans in the chest. "They reveal your weary heart."

Hans sighed. Indeed he was weary. How much longer could he endure the increased taxes placed upon his family? "I tire of unjust rules, that is true. But even you live peaceably, except for converting many souls. Why do you take such risks if you care for the lives of your children?"

"Because people are dying and going to hell for their lack of faith." Martin leaned toward him, his mouth inches away from Hans's ear. "Salvation is by faith, the Scriptures proclaim it. One cannot gain entrance into Heaven by ritual acts enforced by an abbot who cheats the poor."

Hans stepped away. "You must not speak of such." Martin was right though. Hans had found his way into the library at St. Gall just two days ago. Was risky, but what he found there—*hoo*, if it weren't the truth he'd be a knave. The manuscripts spoke of God's grace. He'd heard of such from those Martin had converted. These writings all but convinced him. Indeed they had persuaded him that his sins were paid for by Christ. But to risk his family by joining the Anabaptists? That would be foolhardy.

A twig snapped behind him. Martin ducked behind the bush, and Hans turned with measured intent. "Marlott. You are about early this morning."

"As are you." Sheriff Marlott tugged on his belt surrounding his thick abdomen. "Martin Burger, best you show your face or one might think you are a conspirator."

Martin eased himself from the bush and stretched to his full height while squaring his shoulders in defiance. "It's not against the law to meet with a friend, now is it?"

"Only if the purpose is to convert that friend." Marlott's eyes narrowed. "You are greedy for souls, that I know."

"On the contrary, Sheriff, souls are hungry for Truth. The Truth found in those manuscripts you so well guard in the abbot's library."

Hans laid a hand on Martin's shoulder. The man was too outspoken for his own good. "We are here to make an exchange."

Sheriff Marlott lifted his eyebrow and looked about the area. "I see nothing here. What, pray, do you plan to exchange?"

A lump settled in Hans's throat. He steepled his fingers together then tapped them against his lips. "Information."

Martin's brow puckered. He appeared to be as confused as the sheriff.

Hans lowered his hands and waved his hand in the direction of his farm. "Information on . . . cultivation." That should satisfy the sheriff's curiosity, shouldn't it?

Marlott snorted. "What kind of cultivation?" He drew his pistol. "I think we'll take this up with the court magistrate."

Hans felt the cold fingers of the State encircling his heart. He rubbed his chest.

"There's no need for that, now. We're peaceful people." Martin's forehead bore drops of sweat. "I have six children. I wish not to bring them harm."

Hans massaged the back of his neck.

Marlott seemed to ponder Martin's statement. "I know you to be peaceable, I cannot deny that." He returned the pistol to his belt and pointed to the city across the river. "I have watched you, these last two years, walk through the streets of Berne, and I am aware of your good life." The sheriff's eyes took on a faraway look. An almost wistful look.

Hans fully understood the depth of it, as he knew himself to take on such a look at times when he sought the peace he saw in Martin and his friends.

"If it were up to me . . ." Marlott took a deep breath. "Well, you've done no harm, but Freshling will not be in favor of leaving you be. He'd insist you be put into prison until you could appear before the magistrate."

The chill of the morning took on an edge at the mention of that man. Hans rubbed his thighs, which tingled from the cold. Sheriff Freshling, from across the river, indeed would suffer them to be punished. "You're a just man, sir."

"I advise you to return to your homes." Marlott waved his hand and turned. "Just last Monday Freshling arrested two of your faith, Martin, and tomorrow they will be sent to Venice as galley slaves. I'd not like to see the same for you." He walked away, his boots crunching the snow.

Hans swallowed the lump in his throat as the sheriff turned down the road to the next farm. "Martin, you may use my cave if you will let my family join yours." He might be a fool, but not so big a fool as to not recognize where true peace lay, and it was not with the State Church.

Martin grabbed Hans's hand. "We'd be honored. Quickly now. We've much to gather. Who knows when the wrath of the abbot will come down upon us?"

With a curt nod, Hans fell into step with the Anabaptist. He was into it now. How could he continue to believe the god of the State Church? He snorted. Their god was the god of their bellies. No. If those manuscripts bore truth, and indeed he believed they did, they bore witness to the same God of the Anabaptists. That was the God he wished to serve. A God who saved men on the merit of their faith in Him.

A white rabbit scuttled out of the bush and raced for the field. Its actions startled a small herd of sheep which scattered in every direction. Martin nodded toward them and grimaced. "I fear we will become like those sheep if our leadership does not remain strong."

The sun began to warm Hans's back as he headed toward his farm. "I know that I'm not as good as you. Doubt I'll ever be." Hans swatted the air in the direction of the church steeple that poked the sky across the river. "I know this much. I'll never be good in the abbot's eyes." *For by grace are ye saved through faith; and that not of yourselves: it is the gift of God.* The verse had haunted him these past two days. Nothing he could do could save him. He must accept this free gift. *Lord, I do…I want to receive what You have freely given.* "I…I confess now, as you said earlier. I believe the only way to true salvation is through faith in Jesus Christ." He glanced to the sky. "Lord, please take me. I'm Yours."

A beam of sunlight touched the snow on a fencepost sending a flash of light into the cold air.

He swiped a tear from his eye. "Is there any reason why I cannot be re-baptized? That is what you require, is it not, to be a member of your…ah…church?"

A broad grin spread across Martin's face. "As the apostle Philip answered the Ethiopian Eunuch, "If thou believest with all thine heart, thou mayest."" He laid his hand on Hans's shoulder. "Do you believe that Jesus Christ is the Son of God?"

Hans chuckled. "I've not heard of this eunuch, but if all he needed to do to be saved was believe, then I am like him. I do believe that Jesus Christ is the Son of God." Had not that been made clear in those manuscripts?

"Then perhaps when the weather warms and the river thaws, you can be baptized and become one of us." Martin squeezed his shoulder then struck out across the snow.

Hans smiled and warmth filled his belly. Perhaps he had found that peace Martin spoke of earlier. With a short nod of his head, he glanced at his new brother. Yes, indeed his soul lifted from the fear of death the abbot held over men and drifted on a cloud of peace.

Food For Thought

1. The Bible clearly states that we are saved by grace, yet many people attempt to manipulate God through works. What are some of these works?

Read I Timothy 4:1–8.

"Now the Spirit speaketh expressly, that in the latter times some shall depart from the faith, giving heed to seducing spirits, and doctrines of devils;

Speaking lies in hypocrisy; having their conscience seared with a hot iron;

Forbidding to marry, and commanding to abstain from meats, which God hath created to be received with thanksgiving of them which believe and know the truth.

For every creature of God is good, and nothing to be refused, if it be received with thanksgiving:

For it is sanctified by the word of God and prayer.

If thou put the brethren in remembrance of these things, thou shalt be a good minister of Jesus Christ, nourished up in the words of faith and of good doctrine, whereunto thou hast attained.

But refuse profane and old wives' fables, and exercise thyself rather unto godliness.

For bodily exercise profiteth little: but godliness is profitable unto all things, having promise of the life that now is, and of that which is to come."

I Timothy 4:1–8

What type of exercises do people do in order to appear godly?

2. Can we, by good works, convince God to save us?

"But we are all as an unclean thing, and all our righteousnesses are as filthy rags; and we all do fade as a leaf; and our iniquities, like the wind, have taken us away."

Isaiah 64:6

For centuries, people believed that if they baptized their infants in the church they could influence God to choose to save that child. In some cases they believed their children would be saved because of the baptism, and for others they believed it was entering into a covenant with God. No matter the thinking, their efforts could not guarantee their babies a place in Heaven.

Many people attempt to influence God to bless them on earth by performing good works: feeding the poor; helping the sick or the lame; building homes for the homeless; etc. While all of these things are good and should not be left undone, they do not save a person's soul.

3. What must we do to be saved? The Philippian jailor asked the same question of Paul and Silas in Acts 16:30. How did Paul and Silas respond?

> "And they said, Believe on the Lord Jesus Christ, and thou shalt be saved, and thy house."
>
> Acts 16:31

Study Romans 10. Salvation does not require us to exercise certain traditions or rituals. We do not need to be baptized as infants or drink the sacramental wine. We do not need to pray to Mary or perform pilgrimages. We simply need to repent from our present way of thinking and believe the plain statements of Scripture—believe that Jesus, the Son of God, died for our sins, was buried, and rose again.

THE TIDES OF HATE

Small City, California in the future

Pastor Joseph Conran pulled himself away from the church foyer window and wiped the cold sweat from his brow. "How long Lord, before You return and take us home to live with You? If You came today, You'd spare us such pain."

Brother Clarke had loaded the last of the supplies on the semi-truck, and now the congregation could depart at any moment. Depart for a place where they could worship in truth, without fear of retaliation.

This should give Conran some sense of peace and safety, but instead he felt as though he had given up. *Dear Lord, keep us safe.*

Silence met his prayer.

He picked up the remote and flicked on the television that hung on the back wall of the church foyer, not that he needed to listen to more bad news. "Am I running, Lord?"

The station switched from a commercial to a brunette anchorwoman. "The president just signed the freedom of religion amendment. Many groups who have lobbied for this amendment have planned celebration parties in cities across the country." Her eyes gleamed as she continued. "As of today, people have the freedom to believe what they will, but cannot practice proselytizing or congregating if their particular faith upholds any prejudice or perceived prejudice against any other group. The doors of hundreds of fundamental evangelical churches across the nation have closed already, and now many others will be locked for good. This is a great victory for all those civil rights groups who fought for the liberty of all people, no matter their life choices."

Pastor Conran's shoulders rounded. How often had he encouraged his people to not view this as a defeat? And yet, that was exactly how he felt, defeated.

The scene on the television switched to an old church in downtown Carson City. "This morning, Pastor Cotton of Carson City's First Baptist Church was arrested for encouraging his congregation to continue harboring the useless, the sick, and the elderly chosen for humane termination."

Conran's fists clenched. Last week a pastor in San Francisco had been beaten to death by a hate-filled mob in front of his church. Did those who killed him get arrested? No. The judge called it "a citizen's arrest and an unfortunate accident." What had this country come to?

The foyer door opened, and a whiff of lavender drew him around.

Memories of tear-filled nights on his knees beside his wife, Mary, charged his mind. For how many months had they begged God to change the minds of those who opposed them? *How much longer, Lord, before You return?*

Mary passed through the door. He gave her a wan smile.

"Brother Wayne's ship has docked. He's ready to be loaded. And Señor Garcia called. He said the shacks are up on Quattro Isle, but the solar panels haven't arrived yet."

Conran rubbed his knuckles.

Quattro Isle, the final frontier, a small deserted island in the South Pacific.

He sighed. Years ago, it was the type of destination every American longed for, but under these circumstances…"The people in this country"—he rubbed a pang in his chest—"someone needs to tell them. If we leave, who will tell them?"

Mary rested her hand on his arm. Her mouth smiled, but her eyes did not. "He that reproveth a scorner getteth to himself shame: and he that rebuketh a wicked man getteth himself a blot." She took a deep breath. "We've prayed. God has provided. The deacons agree, and the true members are rallying around us. Leaving is the only thing left for us to do."

"But we could still have a witness. Brother Jacque has chosen to move his church underground—"

"Like the churches in Russia over a hundred years ago."

Conrad nodded.

"But many who could leave Russia did. Do you think that was wrong?" She rubbed his arm, her touch gentle and reassuring.

"No. But I still feel as though I failed."

A siren wailed in the distance, and Mary gripped his arm.

He covered it with his own. "Take Kyla out of here. Don't tell me where. Off the property, if possible."

Her terrified gaze penetrated his. "Kyla won't be able to move quickly enough in her condition."

Conran locked his jaw. Already well past her due date, she could barely maneuver between rooms. "Go, and God be with you." He gave her hand a quick squeeze then pushed her away.

The police car sprang over the approach to the parking lot and screeched to a halt before the church steps.

Conran rubbed the sweat off his upper lip then strode through the front doors as the officers emerged from their vehicle. "Can I help you, gentlemen?"

The older one rested his hand on his gun and jutted his chin toward the semi. "I see you are getting ready to close up."

"As I understand it, we have until Sunday to vacate." Conran swallowed a huff.

The church owned the property, but now that the congregation had been declared a promoter of hatred, its properties had been confiscated...the church had become the victim of society's hatred—a society that claimed they were winning the battle against religious bigotry.

The younger officer pulled off his hat, exposing a shock of blond hair. "I believe your daughter, Kyla Jones, is here."

"I do not know where she is." Could the man see the throbbing artery in Conran's neck?

The officer lifted a paper to Conran's face. "I have a warrant for her arrest."

"What are the charges?" He didn't need to ask, but if he could stall them, perhaps the girls could get away.

"For not aborting her Down Syndrome fetus."

"Baby."

The officer leaned forward. "Pardon me?"

Conran's hands shook. "A fetus is a baby."

The older officer rested a hand on the younger one's shoulder. "We'll not get into that now." He turned to Conran. "You know the penalty for harboring a fugitive."

"I do, but I did not think I was."

"Your daughter's fetus was diagnosed with Down Syndrome. By law, such fetuses are to be aborted to reduce the strain on the medical system."

Heat rose in Conran's face. He clasped his hands behind his back to keep from using them in a manner that would only cause further trouble. "Since she is not here, you will have to look elsewhere."

"Do you mind if we search the premises?"

Conran's cheek twitched. How polite of them to ask. Like he had any choice. "The place is yours." *Lord, please hide Mary and Kyla.*

A Ford Excursion, driven by Brother Clarke, pulled up beside the police car. His eyes met Conran's, and the message conveyed: mobilize.

As the policemen entered the building, Conran moved down the steps. *God, be with us.*

"Is the bus loaded?" Conran asked as Clarke stepped out of the vehicle.

"All six families are on and waiting for the signal." Clarke stood like a marine waiting for orders. Indeed, his military training was an asset. Efficient, unemotional, capable of developing great strategies, God be thanked.

Conran looked back at the church. The brick siding could bear witness to a history of fellowship and love. He rubbed his hand around a smooth column that held up the awning. How many times had he rested against it, visiting with strangers and friends? What would become of it now? His stomach churned. Would they desecrate it as the Babylonians did Solomon's Temple? Heaven forbid it become an abortion clinic.

"Say the word, and I'll hook up the tractor to the trailer."

"Are we giving up?" Conran stared at the pinnacle.

"No." Brother Clarke's tone sobered. "You have a flock that needs you. Within that flock are young children who will need a solid teacher."

"Their parents—"

"Their parents need you."

Conran sighed and dropped his chin to his chest. "I was called to preach the Gospel."

"So preach it to your grandson, and to my grandchildren." Brother Clarke grunted. "And to the natives in the islands around Quattro Isle." He rested his hand on Conran's shoulder. "We don't know what God has planned, but we do know that we've prayed and agreed, and God has made it possible."

But knowing that did not make leaving any easier. They had failed. If they had worked harder, tried more ways, somehow…

"There are others who are staying behind that are better equipped to carry on the work here in the U.S." Brother Clarke opened the passenger door to the Excursion. He lowered his voice. "Mary and Kyla have made it to the bus. We need to leave now, before they are detected."

Lord, I am not running…am I? This is my flock, my daughter, my grandson. You said we must take care of our own family. Conran's gaze swept the church grounds. *How did it get so bad? Why could we not change the tide of hate in this country?*

Brother Clarke's hand squeezed Conran's shoulder. "We are doing the right thing. The time for regrets is past. Perhaps we could have been better witnesses, but we can't change that now. God has given us a new beginning."

"There shouldn't be any need for new beginnings."

"If we do not leave now, we might all be as your son-in-law."

Conran lurched in a cough. Terrence had been shot protecting his wife, Conran's daughter.

His iPhone vibrated in his pocket, and he drew it out then looked at the number. "Brother Jacque."

"I sensed, as I prayed, you needed to remember something. God scattered the early church to spread the Gospel to the rest of the world."

Conran closed his eyes while the tension in his shoulders lifted, and he smiled. "Thank you, brother. And thank You, Lord."

"Go, and remember to pray for us."

"I will."

"As the apostles stood, so shall we."

"So shall we."

Conran turned off his phone and met Brother Clarke's gaze. "We go now, and we will not look back."

Food For Thought

1. Given the direction politics and our society has taken these last fifty years, do you think it will be harder for Christians to share the Gospel and live for Christ in the future?

"If the world hate you, ye know that it hated me before it hated you. If ye were of the world, the world would love his own: but because ye are not of the world, but I have chosen you out of the world, therefore the world hateth you. Remember the word that I said unto you, The servant is not greater than his lord. If they have persecuted me, they will also persecute you; if they have kept my saying, they will keep yours also.

But all these things will they do unto you for my name's sake, because they know not him that sent me."

John 15:18—21

"I have given them thy word; and the world hath hated them, because they are not of the world, even as I am not of the world.

I pray not that thou shouldest take them out of the world, but that thou shouldest keep them from the evil.

They are not of the world, even as I am not of the world.

Sanctify them through thy truth: thy word is truth.
As thou hast sent me into the world, even so have I also sent them into the world.

And for their sakes I sanctify myself, that they also might be sanctified through the truth."

John 17:14—19

Many people who claim to be Christians have sought to be friends with the world, discounting the straight teachings of the Bible as things of the past and not applicable today. James 4:4 says, "Ye adulterers and adulteresses, know ye not that the friendship of the world is enmity with God? whosoever therefore will be a friend of the world is the enemy of God."

2. Imagine 300 years ago, when people in England and Europe experienced persecution for believing contrary to the state religion, the struggles the leaders of these people may have felt, knowing the dangers they would face in the New World. If you experienced such persecution today in this country, what would you do?

3. What can we do today to prevent our country from turning further away from God?

TREASURE BE GLORY

Jason scanned the green gardens of his mother's childhood home. The rolling hills, the crumbling stone wall, the tower, and how about that manor behind him. *Hoo*, how he would have liked to have grown up in such a historical place.

"We best hurry, young Jason." Uncle Philip wiped his brow as he trotted down the stone staircase.

Jason nodded. How did the crippled old man manage to keep the ancient English estate going these last few years?

The manor behind them had at one time taken a team of servants to keep it up, but now many rooms were closed, sheets covering the furniture and cobwebs growing in the corners. The gardens, however, looked to have been maintained with great loving care.

Jason's foot twisted on a wobbly stone, and he winced as he tumbled forward. Uncle Philip obviously didn't have time to keep up on repairs. "What time do you expect the appraiser?"

"Oh, it's not the appraiser today." Uncle Philip puffed as he stepped down onto the stone terrace and waved his hand at a tall building about fifty yards away. "The family collection is kept below that tower." He squared his shoulders. "Your mother and I used to play hide and seek in those ruins." The moss and ivy covered tower certainly looked to be a great place for such games.

Jason rubbed his ankle when he stopped beside his uncle. "Who is coming, then? I thought the bank wanted to have the collection appraised before they put the place up for auction."

Uncle Philip struck out across the green as though he were forty years younger. "Mr. Sutton, the curator of the local museum, is coming with Mr. Craighton, the banker." He called over his shoulder, "Come lad, we've got to find that treasure."

"What treasure? I never heard Grandpa mention any treasure." Jason hustled to keep up.

"That's because he never referred to it as that." Uncle Philip stopped on the cobblestones before the tower and dug into his pocket. "He always referred to it as *The Secret*."

Ah, *The Secret*. Jason chuckled. Grandpa would wave his riding crop in the air and say how *The Secret* would save their family some day. "But no one has ever found it."

"Well, someone must have known where it is. They put it there, now didn't they?" Uncle Philip's hand shook as he shoved the old key in the lock and turned it. "My grandfather said it was worth more than the crown jewels. Grandma would laugh and say in her soprano voice, 'Can't you just see me now all get up in a string of rubies and diamonds walking about the pigs as though I were Queen of England?'" Uncle laughed, and his belly jiggled.

"I can imagine Great-Grandma parading about." Jason followed his uncle into the musty tower and coughed. "Has no air been let in here for centuries?"

"Aye boy, it does have a moldy smell to it. Down here though, see…" Uncle pushed on a queer-looking stone with his toe and a great rumble shook the floor.

Jason grabbed the door handle as a portion of the stone floor slid back, revealing an iron staircase below. "Ho! That's something."

"'Tisn't it?" Uncle tripped a switch. The *thunk, thunk* of overhead lights turning on echoed through the stairwell. "I had these lights put in when your mother tumbled down the stairs. She was sixteen and sweet on the electrician's son." He smiled. "Her friendship made it easier on the pocketbook."

"You mean Dad?"

"Yes sir. Your grandpa nearly had a cow over it, but then your mother and father ran off to America. Near broke your grandmother's heart."

"But if they hadn't, they would never have had me." Jason grinned.

Uncle Philip slapped Jason on the back. "That'd be true, nephew, that'd be true. And here you are, a fine strapping young man off to teach the people of Iraq about God. Yes sir. Your grandpa would be proud." He headed down the stairs. "Now enough chitchat. We've got a mystery to solve."

Jason rubbed his hands together. This would be fun.

The bottom of the staircase opened into a large chamber filled with artifacts from nearly every century of England's history.

Jason eased into the room, mouth open and heart swelling. It was a dream room for a history buff such as himself, like stepping into the past. Even the air was filled with the smells of ancient smoke and oils and leather.

In the center of the room stood a brass celestial globe, not unlike one Jason had seen in the Library of Congress. On the desk behind it stood a bronze statue of some Greek woman, a goddess perhaps? The family crest on a wooden shield hung on the wall. The lions appeared ready to devour each other.

"Hoo, what a room." Jason pivoted on his heel, taking in every detail.

"'Tis something isn't it?" Uncle Philip moved past him to the desk. "But it does not contain the treasure."

Jason turned on his heel to survey the jar of gold coins and ingots, the glass case enclosing the Anglo-Saxon scepter and a jeweled sword, and the various weapons hanging on the walls. "This is better than a museum."

Uncle Philip toyed with his watch. "Hence why that curator wants it. Be the claim of a lifetime, if he could get his hands on it."

The room should be preserved as it was. What better location than in a tower of a former lord of the realm? "Why don't you just set this up as a tourist attraction?"

"Wouldn't make enough money. Old manors are as plentiful in England as the heather on the hills. While this is a good collection, I'd not think it would draw enough to make a go of it." His uncle tapped his wristwatch and lifted it up to his ear.

He must be worried about the time. How could they possibly find a treasure that had been sought for years in only a few minutes? "Still, I'd think it would cover some of your expenses. Keep you from losing the manor wouldn't it?"

The old man shook his head. "Not enough to live off. But maybe if we found that treasure."

"What exactly is the treasure?" Jason's mother mentioned going on treasure hunts. She'd told him stories of searching the grounds for ancient relics, then laugh afterward and say that it was just child's play. Still, if it did exist...

"A letter written about five hundred years ago by one of your ancestors is in the old desk." Uncle Philip pulled open a drawer, tugged on a thread, and lifted the back panel off.

Jason peered over his uncle's shoulder. "Mother never mentioned a letter."

Uncle Philip drew out a brittle roll of yellowed paper tied with a leather thong. He carefully unrolled the delicate scroll, revealing ornate writings.

36

Tingling started in Jason's toes and went right up his spine. Wouldn't this be something to share with his college buddies back home? A real treasure. "What does it say?"

The old man pulled his spectacles from his pocket. He lifted the letter up to the light and squinted at the old English writing. "'Tis for all mankind this treasure's preserved. Its guardians gave their lives so that others may know it's great value. Knights trampled upon the souls of some to gain the knowledge found herein, but on this knight did compassion move."

"That's it?" What kind of a message was that?

"Aye, it is." Uncle Philip shuffled to the full plate-armor by the wood shield. "The knight who wore this, 'tis said, stood by John Wycliffe." He pointed his toe to the soleret, or boot. "You're mother found an inscription on the bottom."

Jason got down on his knees and lifted the knight's foot. The armor clanged and wobbled, but his uncle's hand steadied it while Jason read, "Bones dug, crushed and scattered the Pope did hate." He sat back. "That makes absolutely no sense."

"It does, if you know your history." Uncle Philip snorted, and Jason let the armor clattered back into place.

With a shrug, Jason suppressed the desire to bristle at his uncle's comment. A degree in history truly meant nothing when you lived within it as Uncle Philip apparently did. "What history?"

"Several years after John Wycliffe's death, forty-four I think, Pope Martin V felt so threatened by Wycliffe's work that he had the man's bones dug up, crushed, and scattered in the river."

Of course. Why hadn't he remembered that? "Okay, where do we go from here?"

"We never got past that point. I suspect we need to find a river."

The dogs barked above, and Uncle Phillip frowned. "I'm afraid that is Mr. Sutton and the banker. I'll go see."

Jason's uncle tottered up the stairs.

Turning back to the room, Jason scanned the objects. If he could find the next clue, it might unlock the treasure. Maybe there'd be a priceless jewel or two they could sell. But would that be enough to save the family's estate? "Something about a river . . . is there something with a river in it?"

In a glass case mounted on the wall hung a cracked map. Would seem likely to have a river, right? Jason moved closer.

At the bottom of the manuscript were small calligraphy letters: *Burned at the stake, 1415*. Who would that be?

Men's voices drifted down the stairwell. The curator and banker must be in the garden above. Jason would have to work quickly if he was to find the treasure before they arrived.

He rubbed his chin. Of course. John Hus was burned at the stake for promoting Wycliffe's ideas. He leaned closer and studied a line representing a river. The word "Swift" was written beside it, and beneath that: *The greatest treasure used as kindling, yet God preserved.*

"God preserved." He stepped back. "God preserved what? The treasure?" This still didn't bring him any closer to it.

Scratches, like a key in a lock, came from above.

"They must be entering the tower. Lord, help me." The clues, if he guessed right, seemed to having something to do with the reformers. Wycliffe, John Hus, who came next?

On the wall beside the map was a painting of St. Paul's Cathedral, London. Would that be connected? Again, he scanned the room and held his breath. Was it possible that each artifact held some kind of symbol relating to Christianity?

He snatched up the statue of the Greek woman and turned it over. A fish engraved on the bottom, the symbol used by early Christians to identify themselves. The brass celestial globe had a cross at the top. The weapons bore the symbols of crusaders. The center of the family crest formed a cross.

Scratching his head, he turned back to the painting of the cathedral. What was significant about that Cathedral? John Colet, of course. He was the Dean at St. Paul's, and he read the New Testament in Greek and translated it to English.

The tower door scraped open. "Are you sure you gentlemen wouldn't like tea first?"

"No, no. Busy man now, Philip. I'm a busy man."

Jason pressed his hands against his head. Who came after John Colet?

Erasmus. But what artifact would represent him?

In the far corner a book sat on a round table. Jason hurried across the room. He opened the book and found the imprint of *John Froben*, the man who printed Erasmus's Greek-Latin parallel New Testament. Jason leaned against the table.

A knocking sound came from behind the wall.

"We'll not be long, I hope." One of the men with Uncle Philip spoke. They were coming down the stairs.

Jason pushed the table again. Nothing happened. He picked up the book and the table shifted again. Jason pushed against it, and the wall turned.

A secret passage.

Could Grandpa's Secret be down it?

"Oh my, what wonderful artifacts. Philip Rogers, how could you keep this from the general public?"

Jason slipped through the opening. The cold air smelled earthy, and there appeared to be a long corridor.

"Why this scepter, it could be worth thousands."

"You'll need a government grant to purchase these, I surmise." Uncle was no doubt stalling for him.

Jason pulled a flashlight from his pocket and pressed his hand against the stone wall. He must hurry. Lord willing, the treasure would be down the corridor.

"Yes, indeed. But that would not be difficult."

Feet shuffled.

"Just look at this spectacular painting of…"

The voices faded as Jason moved through the cold hall.

His flashlight cast a glow on a picture of William Tyndale burning at the stake in 1536, another of Martin Luther, and he halted at one of Henry VIII. Beneath that painting stood a podium encased in glass. On the podium lay a book.

Jason lifted his flashlight to read the inscription: *Matthew's Bible, printed by John Rogers, 1537.* Another martyr, Rogers was burned by Mary I in 1554. This indeed was valuable.

If he recalled correctly, there were fewer than three thousand copies made. While this could bring a good price, it still wasn't a treasure of great value.

The Bible was opened to the book of Matthew with a sliver of wood pointing to a passage.

Again, the kingdom of heaven is like unto treasure hid in a field; the which when a man hath found, he hideth, and for joy thereof goeth and selleth all that he hath, and buyeth that field.

Interesting.

"Oh, look at this! A secret passage. Philip, you never told me anything about this." The men had found the entrance.

Not much time now. Jason continued down the corridor. A picture of John Calvin, and one of John Knox, with another Bible, the Geneva Bible, beneath it. Completed 1560. This too would be valuable, and it was opened to Matthew 13 with a toothpick-like marker pointing to:

Again, the kingdom of heaven is like unto a merchant man, seeking goodly pearls:

But this still couldn't be what they were seeking.

Next came the Bishop's Bible, and at the end of the corridor stood one more book beneath a painting of King James I, opened to Matthew 13 and the marked verse:

Who, when he had found one pearl of great price, went and sold all that he had, and bought it.

But could all these originals be enough to cover the amount Uncle Philip owed the bank?

"An original! Indeed a great value."

Jason turned to see a middle-sized man with a blond curly beard scrutinize the Matthew's Bible through a magnifying glass. Was he the curator?

"Such a collection. What great treasures. I say, I do say."

Uncle Philip caught Jason's attention. His eyes twinkled. "Gentlemen, I want to introduce to you my nephew, Jason Aitken. He is on his way to the mission field and has stopped to visit me."

Jason could see the greed in the curator's eyes. He nodded to the gentlemen, trying his best not to reveal his disappointment. The treasure they were looking for was not to be found, at least not in this corridor. And it looked like it was too late.

"Our family has passed down a story about a great treasure. My nephew, you see, has found it."

"I have?"

"Yes, dear nephew. The greatest treasure is also the greatest story. The story of God's love expressed through His redemption of mankind. By finding these old books you have uncovered the history of the preservation of that story. The story of how God came to earth as a man, Jesus Christ; how He died on the cross, was buried and rose again for the forgiveness of sins."

A serenity settled down upon them. Even the curator's face softened. The banker's feet shuffled, almost as if he were uncomfortable.

Dare Jason believe the banker was under conviction?

Uncle Philip wrapped his arm around Jason's shoulder and gave him a rough hug. "Now you will go to your mission field and carry on this legacy. Are you prepared to give your life for Him?"

Jason smiled. Uncle Philip was right. The Gospel message was the greatest treasure. And that corridor revealed the preservation of God's Word and bore witness of the lives given to do so. "Yes, as those before me have. And I will share the wealth."

"Good man."

Still, this find did not keep the estate in the family. "Uncle, what of you and the manor?"

Mr. Craighton, the banker, cleared his throat. "If I might say, I believe we should keep this collection intact in this location. A marvelous tunnel of time, this is. A real bit of history here and a good adventure finding it, too. I'm sure we can convince the government to provide funds to preserve these buildings as a national monument. What do you say Mr. Sutton?"

A grin spread across Jason's face.

"Yes, yes. Quite right. Quite right. A good bit of history and in a nice setting. It could be an extension of our museum. Perhaps Mr. Rogers could act as caretaker?"

Jason tapped his finger against his thigh, hardly containing his excitement.

Uncle Philip beamed. "I'd like nothing better." He raised his hand. "I knew God would find a way to protect His treasure."

Giving his uncle a rough hug, Jason shouted, "Hallelujah!" What a blessing to be able to carry on the tradition of taking God's Holy Word to the lost in Iraq.

Food For Thought

1. If you lived during Tyndale's lifetime, would you have considered him sane? In our small human minds, we tend to think of the preservation of life only in terms of the years we live on earth. However, God sees eternity, and I believe those who became martyrs focused on eternity as well. One day, when we step out of this life and into eternity, we will

be able to speak with John Hus and William Tyndale who died for what they believed. The Apostle Paul said:

> "For I know that this shall turn to my salvation through your prayer, and the supply of the Spirit of Jesus Christ, according to my earnest expectation and my hope, that in nothing I shall be ashamed, but that with all boldness, as always, so now also Christ shall be magnified in my body, whether it be by life, or by death."
>
> Philippians 1:19–20

2. How did we receive the Bible?

> "For the prophecy came not in old time by the will of man: but holy men of God spake as they were moved by the Holy Ghost."
>
> II Peter 1:21

The Bible wasn't made by men, however men of God wrote the Bible, and God, the Holy Ghost, authored it. God preserved His Word through the ages so that we today can read His actual words.

> "The words of the LORD are pure words: as silver tried in a furnace of earth, purified seven times. Thou shalt keep them, O LORD, thou shalt preserve them from this generation for ever."
>
> Psalm 12:6–7

> "Heaven and earth shall pass away, but my words shall not pass away."
>
> Matthew 24:35

3. How can we strengthen our faith so that we can live and die like the martyrs of old? First, we need to be certain we have the faith of the Son of God.

> "I am crucified with Christ: nevertheless I live; yet not I, but Christ liveth in me: and the life which I now live in the flesh I live by **the faith of the Son of God**, who loved me, and gave himself for me."
>
> Galatians 2:20

Second, we need to walk in obedience.

> "And the work of righteousness shall be peace; and the effect of righteousness quietness and assurance for ever."
>
> Isaiah 32:17

When we read and study God's Word, our faith is fed. When we pray and worship we are refreshed as though drinking from a fountain of good water. When we walk in obedience, our faith is strengthened because we see God's Word at work.

CHOICES

Judith pressed her locker door shut then licked her lips in anticipation of her mom's world-famous cheesecake, which her mother promised her as a special treat as soon as she got home from school. Life was good.

A tug on her sleeve pulled her around to see Tyrene's cocky smile beneath a navy blue cowboy hat.

One of Judith's books slipped, and she pushed it back into her arm. Her face heated. "I'm such a klutz."

Tyrene laughed and nodded. "Why don't you come down to the Fort with us?" She shoved her gloved hands into her silver and gray rodeo coat.

Judith lifted the corner of her mouth in a halfhearted smile. "Well..." She shoved back the notion that she was about to be tested.

"I'll teach you how to play pool." Tyrene leaned forward. "And introduce you to that cute cowboy I was telling you about."

Judith hugged her schoolbooks and looked down at her shoes. Her mother may have given her permission to join the High School Rodeo Club, but she didn't think it included joining certain members at the Fort. "I don't know."

Tyrene wrinkled her nose. "Why not?"

Here it came again. That heart-pounding sensation, denying Judith any peace whenever she had to say no to someone. "I…that is, my mother…well, I didn't drive today, so I need to go home on the bus." There, it was said. And it was truthful, too.

"Well, next time you drive, you come to the Fort with us, okay?" Tyrene smiled, though her eyes didn't. She ambled down the corridor to join the rodeo gang at the end of the hall.

"Okay," Judith mumbled. But she shouldn't have said it. It wasn't okay, and she knew it. Her parents would never let her go to what her father described as a "drug haven." She flashed a tight smile at Tyrene's back.

"Hey, Judith." Joe Bishop bumped her arm.

She nodded to him and sighed. Joe was a good guy, really. Just not what the rodeo club girls would consider good-time material. But she really shouldn't knock him for that.

"I was wondering if you'd like to catch a ride home with me. Dad said it would be okay, and I know how you hate to ride the bus."

His goofy grin extruded a chuckle from her. There'd be no harm, but… "Mom's expecting me to come home on the bus."

"Why don't you call her and ask?"

Judith halted the roll of her eyes. "Joe, we've been over this before. Mom doesn't like me to ride home alone with boys. And Dad, well, I'd hate for you to meet him at the door."

Joe nodded. "Yeah, guess you're right. Sorry for you, though. They don't let you do much, do they?"

A snort escaped before Judith could contain it. Sometimes it did seem like they were squelching her style. "Listen, Joe, I know it seems that way, and I admit I don't always like it, but you know what Pastor Buckam says…"

"Obey your parents." He gave her a half smile. "I hear you." With a wave of his hand, he headed for the school exit.

Judith rested her chin on her books. Just once, she wished she could go out with a guy, be a normal girl. She turned on her heel and headed to her bus. Maybe, if she talked to her mom about feeling left out of things, added a few shed tears…maybe then her mom would consent.

"Judith!"

She turned to see Claudia hustling up to her with arms loaded beyond capacity. She tripped on her shoelace and tumbled forward. Judith caught her elbow before she fell.

"Thanks." Claudia bent to gather a renegade book. "Do you think I could sit with you on the bus?"

"Sure." Judith shrugged her shoulders. Claudia may not be the prettiest girl in school, but she was nice. Besides, it was better than sitting alone wondering what student of misdemeanor would be attached to her. "How was your day?"

"Oh fine. I got an A on my Physics test. Should have gotten an A+, but Mr. White didn't agree with my version of the theory of relativity."

Judith pulled her wrap a little tighter around her shoulders as she climbed up the steps of the bus. She took her seat behind the driver.

"Don't you want to go to the back?"

"Why?"

Claudia blushed. "Well, it's more fun back there. I mean…you know…the guys are back there."

Judith glanced to the rear of the bus and watched Daryl Simons whisper in Carrie Terrance's ear. Carrie blushed and did what Judith would definitely call a swoon. "I don't think it's such a good idea."

"Why not? I mean, I know you don't date…"

Judith's cheeks burned. "No. What does that have to do with it?"

"The guys, they like to…well, it's as good as a date."

Like a mountain-sized boulder, Judith's stomach dropped to her feet. "My mother says to sit behind the driver," she squeaked.

"But…"

"Look, Claudia, you don't need to be treated like that. I mean, respect yourself." Judith squeezed her shaky hands together.

"But it's fun."

"How did you feel the first time it happened? Was it fun then?" Why would the girl expose herself to such?... to be used by those…Judith's skin crawled.

Claudia's face turned bright red. She rubbed her books with her index finger then started down the aisle.

Yes, Judith would like to be favored by a boy. After all, what girl didn't want a Prince Charming? But not to be…a toy. To only play games that would lead to hurt.

Judith stared at the back of the bus driver. She'd never had a boy touch her, and she made a vow before the youth group that she would not kiss until the day of her wedding. *Purity*. That's what it was about. Honoring God with the purity of her body…and with what she said and did. "Claudia."

The girl turned. Her face was as white as a sheet.

"Come sit with me. I thought maybe you could show me how to solve that math problem, you know, the one Mr. Plum had on the board?"

Claudia looked at Daryl Simons, who winked at her and made a rude, suggestive gesture. She looked back to Judith. "Okay. You know, I got an A+ on our last test."

Judith smiled, scooted to the window, and set her books on her lap. "I got a C-. I'm glad you're willing to help."

The color came back to Claudia's cheeks. She lowered herself to the seat and opened a notebook.

"I was wondering. Would you be interested in coming to our youth group Friday night? We're having a hayride at the Brightons' farm."

Claudia nodded. A smile filled her face, and her eyes twinkled. "I thought you would never ask."

Judith laughed. "I never knew you wanted to come." She should have asked a long time ago. "We always have such a good time."

"I've heard." Claudia tapped her notebook with a pencil. "Let's get this done so we can talk about the hayride." Then she dove into the math problem.

Judith's stomach no longer represented a boulder. In fact, she felt quite light and free—she took a deep, relaxing breath—and very happy to have made some good choices.

"My son, if sinners entice thee, consent thou not." Proverbs 1:10

Food For Thought

1. How would you define purity?

> "Let no man despise thy youth; but be thou an example of the believers, in word, in conversation, in charity, in spirit, in faith, in purity."
>
> I Timothy 4:12

The Greek word used in this verse for purity means cleanliness or chastity. In other words: a life without sin.

The problem in today's Christianity is that sin, purity, and chastity have become redefined. Consider the following passage of Scripture:

> "Ye have heard that it was said by them of old time, Thou shalt not commit adultery:
>
> But I say unto you, That whosoever looketh on a woman to lust after her hath committed adultery with her already in his heart."
>
> Matthew 5:27–28

Christ's standard is even higher than that of the Pharisees.

2. What were Judith's parents trying to protect her from? In your Bible read Proverbs 1:10–18.

"Enter not into the path of the wicked, and go not in the way of evil men.

Avoid it, pass not by it, turn from it, and pass away. For they sleep not, except they have done mischief; and their sleep is taken away, unless they cause some to fall.

For they eat the bread of wickedness, and drink the wine of violence.

But the path of the just is as the shining light, that shineth more and more unto the perfect day.

The way of the wicked is as darkness: they know not at what they stumble."

Proverbs 4:14–19

3. How was Judith proving her faith to those around her? In your Bible read I Peter 3:15–18.

"Beloved, think it not strange concerning the fiery trial which is to try you, as though some strange thing happened unto you:

But rejoice, inasmuch as ye are partakers of Christ's sufferings; that, when his glory shall be revealed, ye may be glad also with exceeding joy.

If ye be reproached for the name of Christ, happy are ye; for the spirit of glory and of God resteth upon you:

on their part he is evil spoken of, but on your part he is glorified.

But let none of you suffer as a murderer, or as a thief, or as an evildoer, or as a busybody in other men's matters.

Yet if any man suffer as a Christian, let him not be ashamed; but let him glorify God on this behalf.

For the time is come that judgment must begin at the house of God: and if it first begin at us, what shall the end be of them that obey not the gospel of God?

And if the righteous scarcely be saved, where shall t he ungodly and the sinner appear?"

I Peter 4:12–18

FOR ETERNITY

Carlyle slid across the hardwood floor to Chantelle. To charm her was to defeat her. "Tonight, my dear, the setting sun glistened in your hair, a golden hue richer than the deepest mine in the Sierras."

"Tonight, you will leave off flattery. It will not work."

"Yet, how could I not be entranced by your beauty?"

She looked at his eyes, a cutting look, but no curling the lip, as some might. "Your eyes do not reflect your words." She turned back to the crashing ocean outside the large window, arms crossed and jaw set.

He smiled. She was a dike to be battered, but he should have known by now the armament of charm would not work. "The ocean is filled with creatures, passionate about life." He pushed a stuffed whale across the pine floor. "What are you passionate about?"

She stepped around the whale and pressed her hand against the floor-to-ceiling window. "Eternal life."

He snorted and rubbed the smirk from his face. Eternal life. Has she not seen dead animals? They no longer move. They are forgotten. Gone forever. She should have guessed his view on life, but if he wished to sway her from her mission, if he wished to defeat her cause, then he must remain controlled.

She turned and her angelic face lit with what he knew held her heart, a love for God. Fool. No god worth loving existed.

The storm outside wailed, and the spray from the ocean rained against the glass. He flinched. For all his years along the Monterey Coast, the sea had never been so wild.

"Have you seen the night sky?"

He shot a quick look at the dark, tumbling clouds. "It will rain soon."

"I don't mean right now. I mean on a clear night." She took a step toward him, her face an earnest tale of reckless abandonment to a faith that soured his stomach. "On a clear night the stars hang in an endless background; a universe that man cannot find the end to; a vastness so great, so perpetual that this planet appears little more than a speck of dust."

He moved away. The cold of the pending storm radiated through the pane, yet his heart burned. This woman spoke with the wisdom of the ages each time he encountered her. Nonetheless, if he did not ruin her reputation, destroy her in some way, that wisdom would control the heart of the richest man in the world, William Judd.

He circled her, a hawk above its kill. She stood between him and his dream, dominion over America, and perhaps even the world.

"Yet God made the universe for Earth, because He made Earth for man, whom He created in His image."

Carlyle pressed his hot palm against the cold pane. The wind pressed back and the rain slammed a rhythm of rage against his hand. If he succeeded in convincing William he was his son, he would be heir to an empire greater than the United States of America. But Chantelle had the ear and the heart of this most powerful man. To get to him, Carlyle must go through her.

"Then man turned against Him."

Carlyle shook his head. "What?"

She turned back to the window and placed both hands against the pane above her head. Tears ran down her face as she lifted it to the sky. "Man rebelled against God . . . much as you plan to rebel against the man you want to call Father."

"You could die for words like that." He quelled the urge to smack her.

"And if you did, I would be victorious."

"Not if I'm not convicted. I'd win your husband over. I'd become the heir. Your little Baptist missions group would get nothing."

She lowered her chin to her chest. "That is where you are wrong. If I die, I go to be with the Lord. I will no longer be tormented by men like you. And God can keep the missions group going, for as long as He wills. But Carlyle"—she looked at him, her eyes pools of sorrow—"what you long for you could have, if you surrendered to Christ."

He laughed. This was not the first he'd heard such gibberish. Years ago a masterful speaker grabbed his heart with similar words. "I've asked Jesus to be my friend, my ally. He never did what I asked. My mother died. I lost the financial race of my life. Jesus either doesn't exist or is powerless." But even as he spoke those words his heart defied them.

"You wanted a friend and an ally, but did you recognize that Jesus is holy? That you are a sinner, in need of the salvation He could give you?" She turned her gaze on him, and he shuddered. That gaze was not one of hate, but sorrow. She should hate him for what he was about to do to her and her husband.

Her lips trembled then she said, "And now you lay claim to your father, a mere step to what you think you really want. Yet I stand in your way."

"We could work together, you know. We could rule this world." Why should he feel so earnest to do so? She would drag him down, but if he could entice her with power, what the two of them could do...how they could live...

She shook her head. "What good is it if you should gain the whole world, but lose your soul?" Her fists clenched. "You need to know that how you have lived was wrong, and what you are doing is wrong. If you would only recognize your need and believe in Jesus, in the salvation He offers—"

He slammed his fist against the window. It rattled. A large wave rose above the cliff below and pounded the glass wall. He stumbled back, but Chantelle leaned into the window.

"I have no soul worth saving!" His back muscles convulsed as images of his reckless life accused him.

"When you die, where will you go?"

"Nowhere. That is why I must live for all I'm worth today. That is why I must look after my own interests." He screamed at her, but the wind screamed louder.

The pane shook. Chantelle stood as though holding it in place. He moved farther back.

"You are deceived."

Did she say that, or the wind? If he were honest, if he listened to his innermost thoughts…but he mustn't. If he did, he would surrender. If he surrendered, his wants and desires would not be met.

The floor shook as another foamy crest pounded against the picture window. Chantelle whispered, "We've got to get out of here. I've never seen the waves so high."

He headed for the door, but the glass broke. Water crashed in, pulling his feet out from beneath him. "Chantelle!" He swept by her as the floor shifted under the water.

She grabbed his arm. "Hang on!"

Water filled his mouth and covered his eyes. Dark. Cold. It went away. He gasped.

The floor crashed. Chantelle clung to the window frame and he to her. Another wave rose over them like a monster about to devour. It crashed down.

He swallowed the salty water and hungered for air.

Pain in his chest.

Was there eternity?

Pain increased.

It had to stop.

Pain intensified.

Would this last an eternity?

He pulled on Chantelle. His grip slipped.

Darkness. Screams.

Something grabbed his shirt collar. It dragged him through the water. He should grab hold. His arms wouldn't work. God help him. *Forgive me, Lord.*

"Carlyle." Her voice, a million miles away.

Was he dead? Hell awaited him, he was sure of that. *No, God, I believe. I choose to believe. I need your salvation.*

"Carlyle." A light broke through.

Where did it come from? Would God save him?

His body thumped down hard.

He gagged.

Someone pulled him onto his side.

Water poured from his mouth.

"Carlyle." Her lavender perfume infused the air that rushed into his lungs.

He coughed and breathed again. "Chantelle."

"I'm here and so is your father."

"You saved me?" He stared at her wet clothes. She sat beside him on the foyer floor.

"She dove in after you. I thought I lost you both." William's deep, rumbling voice sliced through the cold air. Above them, the wind continued to roar.

Was he accusing Carlyle? "Would you care if you did?"

"Yes, son."

Son? Did William finally believe he was his son? But Carlyle felt suddenly weak. He should be smiling, but instead he wanted to weep. He should rejoice. He was scum.

"The ambulance is on the way." Chantelle touched his shoulder. "Think about your place in eternity. We want you to be there with us."

Sirens wailed above the storm's rumble.

William's son. Carlyle had gained the world. Did he lose his soul? "Chantelle?"

"Yes."

"How does one surrender to Christ?"

"Have faith in the One who died for you. Then, give up the world, deny yourself, take up His cross, and follow Him."

> "Then said Jesus unto his disciples, If any man will come after me, let him deny himself, and take up his cross, and follow me. For whosoever will save his life shall lose it: and whosoever will lose his life for my sake shall find it. For what is a man profited, if he shall gain the whole world, and lose his own soul? or what shall a man give in exchange for his soul?"
>
> Matthew 16:24–26

Food for Thought

If after you have read this, you realize your heart is in the same condition as Carlyle's, why not choose to follow Christ?

> "That if thou shalt confess with thy mouth the Lord Jesus, and shalt believe in thine heart that God hath raised him from the dead, thou shalt be saved. For with the heart man believeth unto righteousness; and with the mouth confession is made unto salvation."
>
> Romans 10:9–10

Your heart is your soul, your mind, your emotions. It is the very seat of your thoughts, your passions, affections— where you purpose and mold your will. When you seek after Jesus' with all your heart, you will find Him. When you give your heart over to Jesus, you are submitting your will to Him and to His desires. You cannot do this unless you turn from your present way of thinking and reasoning. That is repentance.

When you reach the point in your life where your passion is for Christ and not for the things of this world, when you seek Him with all your heart, you can call on His name, and He will save you from your sins.

> "For whosoever shall call upon the name of the Lord shall be saved."
>
> Romans 10:13

If you desire to be saved, and you want someone to discuss this with you, email me at lynnsquire@gmail.com, and I'll lead you through Scripture that will tell you how you too can have eternal life.

IF YOU ARE A FAN OF THIS BOOK, PLEASE TELL OTHERS...

- Write about *A Week of Faith More Precious than Gold* on your blog, Twitter, Facebook, or other social media services.
- Suggest *A Week of Faith More Precious than Gold* to friends.
- When you're in a bookstore, ask them if they carry the book.
- Writer a positive review of *A Week of Faith More Precious than Gold* on www.amazon.com, www.goodreads.com, and other online book clubs and stores.
- Send me or Faith Journey Books suggestions on websites, conferences, and events you know of where this book could be offered.
- Purchase additional copies to give away as gifts.

IF YOU ENJOYED THIS BOOK YOU MIGHT ALSO ENJOY:

Joab's Fire

Joab Black and his wife Sarah overcame the worst of pioneer hardships in order to establish a prosperous farm in Alberta, Canada. But those challenges never prepared them for the tragedy they now faced—a staggering loss and intense pain causing them to doubt everything they had ever believed. In the midst of their sorrow, even their closest friends interpret their sufferings as a result of God's judgment. Has God abandoned them?

Sergeant Dixon, the local North West Mounted Police officer, investigates the events leading to the Blacks' plight. While his work gives them a ray of hope, his probing into the activities of a certain stranger possibly connected to the case may cost him his job and even his life.

Inspired by the Biblical book of Job, *Joab's Fire* includes a Bible study exploring the perfection of God's plan and the bounty of His love even in the most inexplicable and intense sufferings.

FICTION / Religious/ 978-1-935245-51-3/ $14.99 / www.ahigherlife.com

Best of Faith, Fiction, Fun, and Fanciful

An anthology of short stories, devotionals and poetry that takes us through the journey of life, its rises and falls, its joy and sorrow, and its moments of revelation.

Come walk with Harry on a tightrope across a snake pit; become a superhero on a haystack; and be inspired by other characters as they journey through life in the pursuit of the most desirable freedom mankind can ever know.

You can order this book from Barnes and Noble, Amazon.com, and other bookstores.

Inspirational Fiction/Poetry/Devotional / 978-143847915 / www.PresentingBiblicalTruths.com

Connect with me…

Visit my blog at:
http://faithfictionfunandfanciful.blogspot.com
and my websites:
www.lynnsquire.com
www.PresentingBiblicalTruths.com.
You may also contact me directly at lynnsquire@gmail.com.

ABOUT THE AUTHOR

LYNN SQUIRE grew up on a farm in Southern Alberta where much of her perspective on life was shaped. As a child, she came to understand who she was in light of a holy God, and that she needed Jesus Christ as her Saviour. This relationship became her life's driving force, as long as she kept "self" out of the way. Nonetheless, God led her through educational valleys, across plains of complacency, and over mountains of life experiences, to her present location, California. She attends Calvary Baptist Church in American Canyon, California, with her husband and three children.